RAPID RIVER RESCUE

JOHN TOWNSEND

QEB

QEB Publishing

Cover Design: Punch Bowl Design
Illustrator: Tatio Viana
Editor: Claudia Martin
Designer: Carol Davis
QED Project Editors: Ruth Symons
and Carly Madden
QED Project Designers:
Krina Patel and Rachel Lawston
Editorial Director: Victoria Garrard
Art Director: Laura Roberts-Jensen

Copyright © QEB Publishing 2015

First published in the United States by
QEB Publishing, Inc.
3 Wrigley, Suite A
Irvine, CA 92618

www.qed-publishing.co.uk

A CIP record for this book is available
from the Library of Congress.

ISBN 978 1 60992 796 7

Printed in China

Picture credits
Shutterstock: Aron Brand 37; bumihills 8;
ETIENjones 13; jejim 38; leungchopan 28;
Mycola Mazuryk 16; narcisse 5, 12, 18,
19, 36; Sam DCruz 21; sittitap 12; Sombat
Khamin 20; sopose 10.

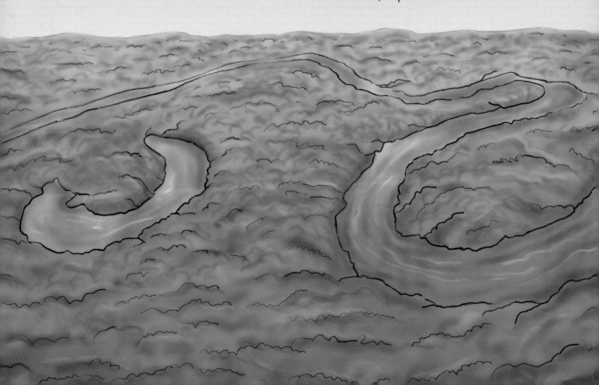

How to begin your adventure:

Are you ready for an amazing adventure that will test your brain power to the limit—full of mind-bending puzzles, twists, and turns? Then you've come to the right place!

Rapid River Rescue is no ordinary book—you don't read the pages in order, 1, 2, 3 . . .

Instead you jump forward and backward through the book as you face a series of challenges. Sometimes you may lose your way, but the story will always guide you back to where you need to be.

The story begins on page 4. Straight away, there are questions to answer and problems to overcome. The questions will look something like this:

| IF YOU THINK THE **CORRECT ANSWER IS A,** GO TO PAGE 10 | A | IF YOU THINK THE **CORRECT ANSWER IS B,** GO TO PAGE 18 | B |

Your task is to solve each problem. If you think the correct answer is A, turn to page 10 and look for the same symbol in red. That's where you will find the next part of the story. If you make the wrong choice, the text will explain where you went wrong and let you have another chance.

The problems in this adventure are about rivers and their features. To solve them, you must use your geography skills. To help you, there's a glossary of useful words at the back of the book, starting on page 44.

ARE YOU READY?
Turn the page and let your adventure begin!

RAPID RIVER RESCUE

You're a world-famous treasure hunter, just home from your latest expedition. You're reading the newspaper, when you receive a mysterious text message:

I want your treasure! If you don't give it to me I'll poison your local river—and everyone who depends on it. You'll have to find me first. I've left a trail of clues for you. Catch me if you can. By midnight. The Toxic Texter.

This is serious. There's not a minute to lose!

TURN TO PAGE 10 TO SAVE THE RIVER

NEWS
TREASURE HUNTER FINDS HIDDEN GOLD

You got it right. You can see a flashing light near a sandy bank on a bend in the river. That must be an alluvium bank.

It's a buoy with a flashing beacon! You climb out of the kayak to read a message that's tied to it:

"You are very close. This buoy is connected to three ropes: A, B, and C. Pull the one that answers this question."

What is a watershed?

AN AREA DIVIDING TWO RIVER SYSTEMS.
TURN TO PAGE 39

 A

A U-SHAPED LAKE.
GO TO PAGE 23

B

A BOAT SHED.
HEAD TO PAGE 36

C

 No, you're thinking of an estuary.

GO BACK TO PAGE 43 AND TRY AGAIN

Incorrect answer. The scary woman says you can't possibly be a real explorer.

TURN BACK TO PAGE 41 AND THINK AGAIN

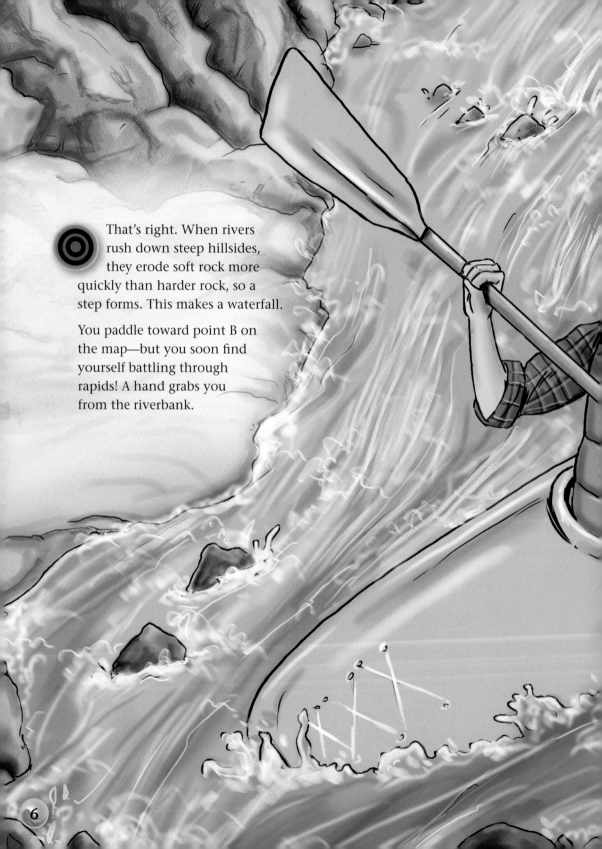

That's right. When rivers rush down steep hillsides, they erode soft rock more quickly than harder rock, so a step forms. This makes a waterfall.

You paddle toward point B on the map—but you soon find yourself battling through rapids! A hand grabs you from the riverbank.

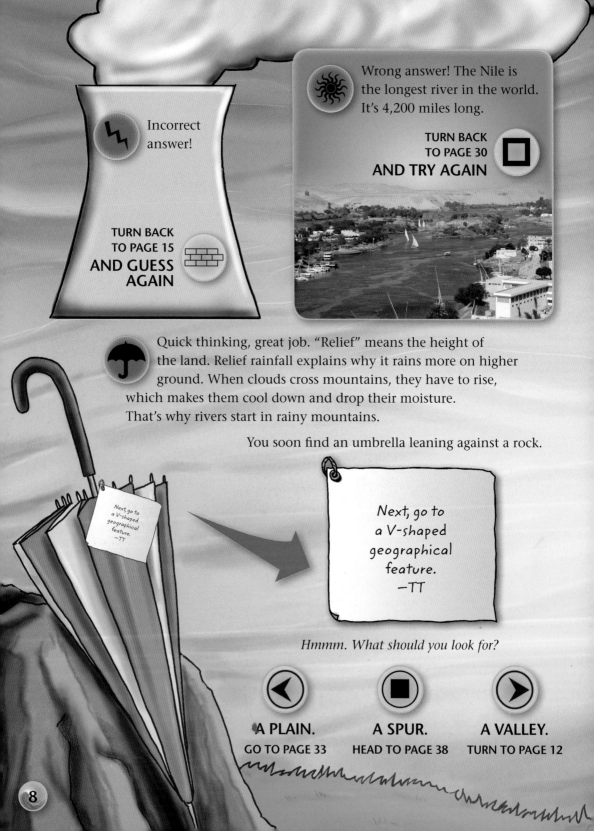

Incorrect answer!

TURN BACK TO PAGE 15 AND GUESS AGAIN

Wrong answer! The Nile is the longest river in the world. It's 4,200 miles long.

TURN BACK TO PAGE 30 AND TRY AGAIN

Quick thinking, great job. "Relief" means the height of the land. Relief rainfall explains why it rains more on higher ground. When clouds cross mountains, they have to rise, which makes them cool down and drop their moisture. That's why rivers start in rainy mountains.

You soon find an umbrella leaning against a rock.

Next, go to a V-shaped geographical feature. —TT

Next, go to a V-shaped geographical feature. —TT

Hmmm. What should you look for?

A PLAIN.
GO TO PAGE 33

A SPUR.
HEAD TO PAGE 38

A VALLEY.
TURN TO PAGE 12

2 That's a dead end. This tunnel passes a column, formed when stalagmites and stalactites join together.

GO BACK TO PAGE 24 AND TRY AGAIN

No. Although we do use rivers for recreation, such as sailing and fishing, that's not what irrigation means.

TURN BACK TO PAGE 42 AND THINK AGAIN

▶ You made the right choice. Angel Falls in Venezuela is the world's highest waterfall, with a drop of 3,200 feet.

You paddle on until you see a fisherman, standing on the bank. To your surprise, he is dangling a piece of paper at you from his fishing rod. It's another map of the river.

(A) (B)
(C)

I have a message for you. Answer this question to find out if you should go to A, B, or C marked on the map. What causes a waterfall?

◆ **A = TOO MUCH WATER.**
GO TO PAGE 12

◎ **B = EROSION OF WEAKER ROCKS.**
TURN TO PAGE 6

◆ **C = A RIVER GETTING CLOGGED UP WITH ROCKS.**
GO TO PAGE 20

You grab your compass and some sturdy boots, then send a text message back: "You villainous monster! If you keep your poison out of the water, I'll pay up. Where do your clues start?"

The reply comes immediately: "Where do you think? At the start of the river!"

What is the start of a river called?

THE MOUTH.
FLIP TO PAGE 18

THE SOURCE.
GO TO PAGE 30

THE BASIN.
TURN TO PAGE 36

No, that's not right. The river water is salty here, but that's because you're close to the sea, not because of alluvium.

GO BACK TO PAGE 21
AND THINK AGAIN

No, that's a reservoir. Now you're facing arrest!

TURN QUICKLY
BACK TO PAGE 31
AND TRY AGAIN

3

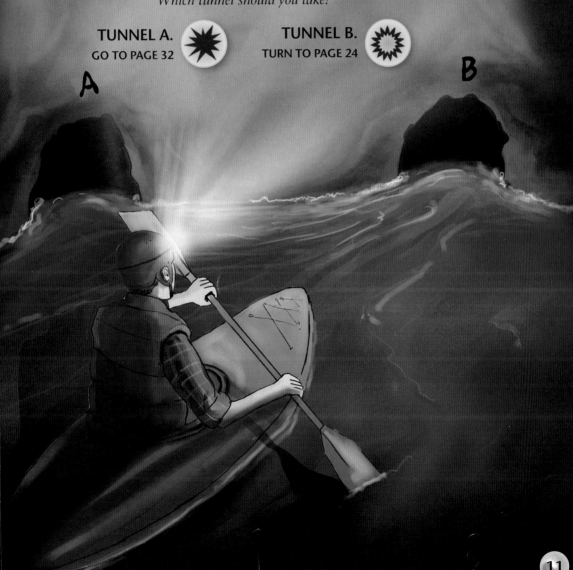

 It's become totally dark—time to switch on the light on your helmet. You're in an underground cave and there's a message written on the wall!

WHAT CAUSED THIS SWALLOW HOLE? IF YOU THINK IT WAS CAUSED BY IMPERMEABLE ROCK, TAKE TUNNEL A. IF IT WAS CAUSED BY PERMEABLE ROCK, TAKE TUNNEL B. TT

Which tunnel should you take?

TUNNEL A.

GO TO PAGE 32

TUNNEL B.

TURN TO PAGE 24

A

B

Correct. As water in the mountains flows downhill, it cuts a channel into the land. Over time, this gradually deepens into a V-shaped valley.

You trudge downstream into the river valley. At last, you find a kayak on the bank, with a clue attached to it.

If I've labeled this diagram of the water cycle correctly, climb into the kayak and start to paddle. If not, carry on walking.
—TT

Water falls from clouds as rain or snow

Water vapor condenses into clouds

Water evaporates from the sea as vapor

Water flows to the sea in streams and rivers

 You've gone the wrong way. This gentle bend is a meander.

TURN BACK TO PAGE 26 AND TRY AGAIN

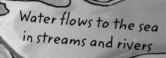

Do you get in the kayak?

NO.
TURN TO PAGE 43

YES.
GO TO PAGE 41

 Wrong choice. It's not the amount of water in a river that causes a waterfall, but the speed, steepness, and eroding power of the river.

TURN BACK TO PAGE 9 AND TRY AGAIN

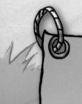

Wrong answer. Soggy marshes are often found at the edges of rivers, but they may have no alluvium at all.

TURN BACK TO PAGE 21 AND TRY AGAIN

 Nope. At the far end of a river, the water flows much more slowly and can create winding valleys across flat plains.

GO BACK TO PAGE 6 AND TRY AGAIN

 That's right. The Grand Canyon was cut over thousands of years by the power of running water and rocks swept along by the river.

I'm still not sure about you. Before I let you paddle on your way, here's another question you must get right: When running water wears down rock along a river's bed and banks, what is the process called?

WEATHERING.
TURN TO PAGE 37

EROSION.
GO TO PAGE 17

SLOSHING.
FLIP TO PAGE 21

Yes, that's exactly right. To escape arrest, you'll have to pretend to be an engineer. You ask the guard to show you the dam.

"Come on then," he bellows. *"Answer this security question to gain clearance to the HEP station. What does HEP stand for?"*

HIGH ENERGY PLANT
FOR CONTROLLING THE RIVER FLOW.
GO TO PAGE 8

HYDROELECTRIC POWER
FOR MAKING ELECTRICITY.
TURN TO PAGE 36

HYDRAULIC ENGINEERING PROJECT
FOR STORING WATER.
HEAD TO PAGE 28

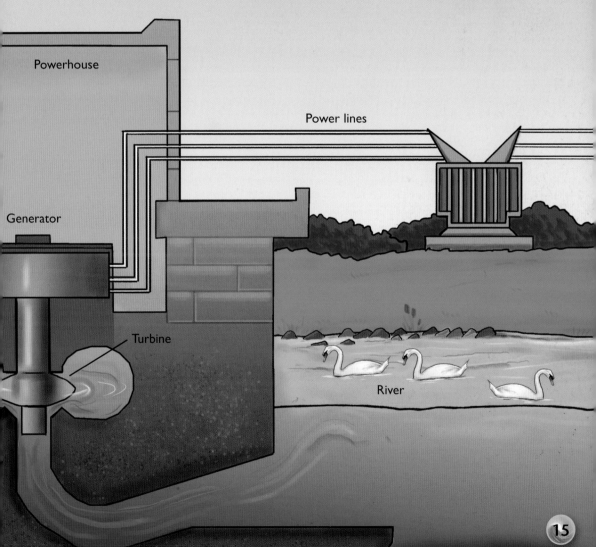

Powerhouse

Power lines

Generator

Turbine

River

That's right, wade in. The bottom of a stream or river is called its bed. It can be rocky or covered by mud. Have a good look at the stream bed.

You soon spot a jar under the water. You open it and pull out a clue:

"You're up in the mountains. What a relief! You're going to need something beginning with U. —TT"

Another riddle! What's the Toxic Texter talking about?

What should you look for?

AN UMBRELLA.
TURN TO PAGE 8

UNDERWEAR.
GO TO PAGE 27

Wrong answer. In the middle part of a river, between its source and the sea, the river flows more slowly. It often creates wide, shallow valleys.

TURN BACK TO PAGE 6
AND TRY AGAIN

Wrong way. Those are stalagmites, which grow up from the cavern floor.

GO BACK TO PAGE 24
AND TRY AGAIN

Phew, that's the correct answer!

"You've passed the test. I'll let you carry on. But look out for the waterfall," the woman shouts over her shoulder.

Yikes! Before you know it, your kayak is dragged over the edge of a waterfall. You nose-dive into a plunge pool, where you see a plastic duck bobbing beside you. There's a message on it:

The river forks here. If the following statement is true, take the left fork. The Niagara Falls are the highest waterfalls in the world.

—TT

Which fork do you take?

LEFT.

TURN TO PAGE 37

RIGHT.

HEAD TO PAGE 9

Don't be silly!

**TURN BACK TO PAGE 28
AND TRY AGAIN**

You've got off to the wrong start! The mouth is at the end of a river, where it empties into the sea or a lake.

**GO BACK TO PAGE 10
AND TRY AGAIN**

Wrong answer.

**GO BACK TO
PAGE 38
AND CHOOSE
AGAIN**

Good choice. Now you're in a gorge with steep rocky sides like a mini canyon.

But suddenly your kayak is spinning around and around. You're caught in a whirlpool and being sucked down into a swirling swallow hole . . .

**TURN TO PAGE 11
TO FIND OUT WHAT'S
HAPPENING TO YOU!**

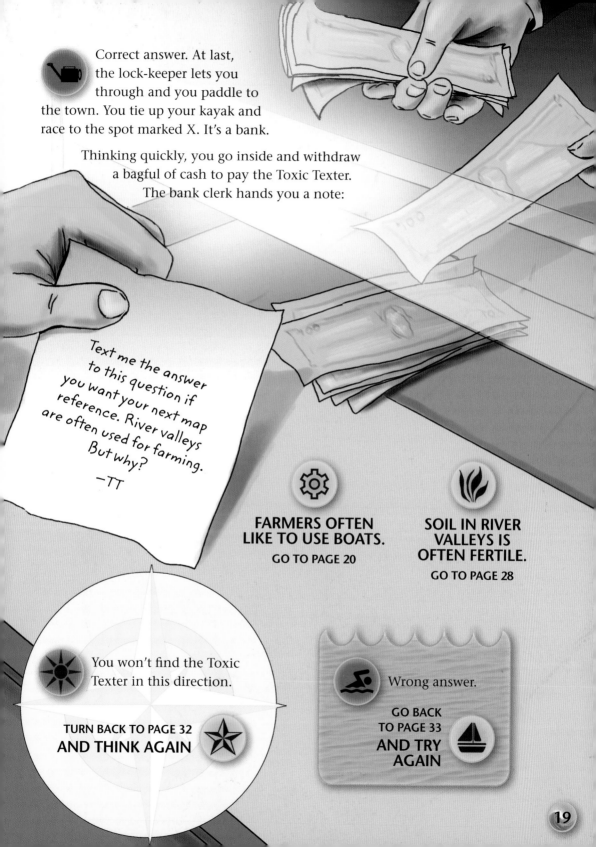

Correct answer. At last, the lock-keeper lets you through and you paddle to the town. You tie up your kayak and race to the spot marked X. It's a bank.

Thinking quickly, you go inside and withdraw a bagful of cash to pay the Toxic Texter. The bank clerk hands you a note:

Text me the answer to this question if you want your next map reference. River valleys are often used for farming. But why?

—TT

FARMERS OFTEN LIKE TO USE BOATS.
GO TO PAGE 20

SOIL IN RIVER VALLEYS IS OFTEN FERTILE.
GO TO PAGE 28

You won't find the Toxic Texter in this direction.

TURN BACK TO PAGE 32
AND THINK AGAIN

Wrong answer.

GO BACK TO PAGE 33
AND TRY AGAIN

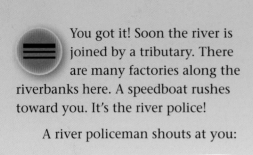 You got it! Soon the river is joined by a tributary. There are many factories along the riverbanks here. A speedboat rushes toward you. It's the river police!

A river policeman shouts at you:

You shouldn't kayak here! Don't you know how dangerous it is? There's terrible industrial pollution in this part of the river. Do you know why?

 That is the wrong answer.

TURN BACK TO PAGE 19 AND TRY AGAIN

FACTORIES ARE POLLUTING THE RIVER WATER.

GO TO PAGE 29

FACTORY SMOKE IS SPOILING THE VIEW.

TURN TO PAGE 41

NOISY FACTORIES ARE DEAFENING EVERYONE.

GO TO PAGE 23

 Nope. Rivers do deposit (drop) material such as rocks, but waterfalls aren't formed that way.

GO BACK TO PAGE 9 FOR ANOTHER TRY

No, that's not a geographical term.

TURN BACK TO PAGE 13 AND TRY AGAIN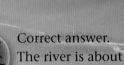

 Wrong answer! The spring isn't a bedspring. Instead it's where water flows to the surface from underground. You won't find the next clue there.

GO BACK TO PAGE 40 AND TRY AGAIN

Correct answer. The river is about to join the sea. It's choppy because the flowing water is mixing with the sea, which constantly rises and falls with the tides.

The police officer speeds off, shouting over his shoulder:

We've had a tip-off. The river is at risk from a supervillain. We've got an address!

Another text comes in.

You've just got one last chance: my hideout is on an alluvium bank. Come and get me!

What's an alluvium bank?

MARSHLAND AT THE MOUTH OF A RIVER.
TURN TO PAGE 13

DEPOSITS LEFT BY FLOWING WATER.
HEAD TO PAGE 5

SALTY RIVER WATER.
GO TO PAGE 10

That's it! A steel door in the wall slides open to reveal a woman. You've seen her before somewhere. Her finger is poised over a button.

I'm the Toxic Texter, but you can call me TT. I've been following you down the river in various disguises.

I was all the people you met along the way—apart from the police, of course. They just arrived to arrest me, but I froze them solid with my liquid nitrogen gun!

I can see you've come empty-handed. That's not good enough. I'm going to release the tank of poison by pushing this button.

THINK OF A PLAN FAST!
TURN TO PAGE 42
TO SAVE THE RIVER

Wrong way!

TURN BACK TO PAGE 32 AND TRY AGAIN

That's not correct. HEP stations don't pollute the water or air.

GO BACK TO PAGE 36 AND TRY AGAIN

That's not the right answer, although noise pollution can be unpleasant.

TURN BACK TO PAGE 20 AND THINK AGAIN

B Wrong rope. You're thinking of an oxbow lake, which can form when a bend in a river is cut off from the main river.

GO BACK TO PAGE 5 AND PULL ANOTHER ROPE

Oxbow lake

River

You picked the correct tunnel. When a stream crosses permeable rock like this limestone, the water trickles through cracks in the rock. Over time, the water can erode a larger and larger hole, until it becomes a swallow hole.

Tunnel B leads to an underground cavern made by water seeping through rock and sweeping away debris over millions of years. But you haven't got time to admire the view—hurry to get out of here.

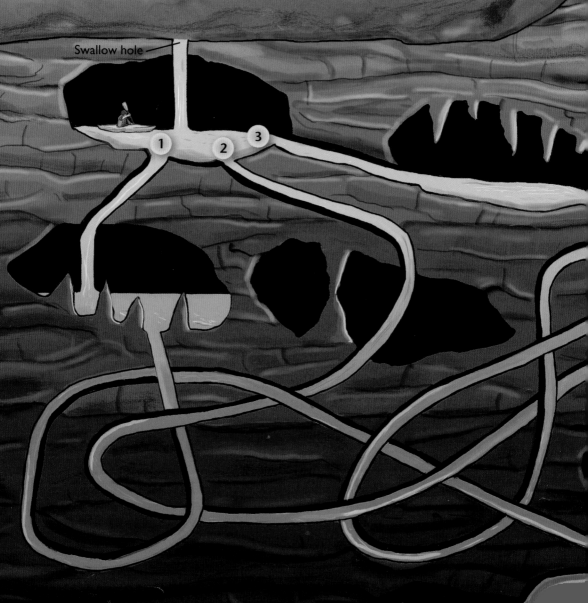

Swallow hole

1   2   3

WAY OUT

A sign says: "*The exit is past the stalactites. —TT*"

Which tunnel leads to the way out?

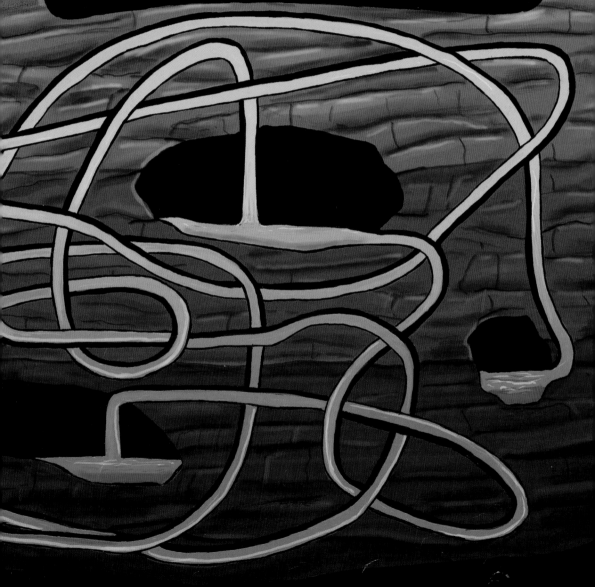

1

TUNNEL 1.

TURN TO PAGE 16

2

TUNNEL 2.

GO TO PAGE 9

3

TUNNEL 3.

FLIP TO PAGE 31

You're right! Rapids are found close to a river's source, where it is fast-flowing and has great energy. The river erodes the soft rock along its bed and leaves ridges of hard rock, creating a very bumpy ride!

All right, you can go on. I've got a message for you from TT: Head for the gorge!

The river is dividing again. On the left fork, the river swings into a gentle bend beside grassy banks. On the right fork, it cuts through a narrow passage in the rock.

Which fork heads into a gorge?

THE LEFT FORK.
FLIP TO PAGE 12

THE RIGHT FORK.
TURN TO PAGE 18

No, that's not a tributary. Pollution from toilets (sewage) and factories is called effluent.

TURN BACK
TO PAGE 43
AND TRY AGAIN

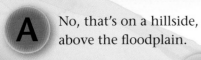

A No, that's on a hillside, above the floodplain.

TURN BACK TO PAGE 30 AND TRY AGAIN

 Wrong choice—although it can get chilly up in the mountains, so let's hope you're wearing your thermals. Remember that the Toxic Texter mentioned "relief."

TURN BACK TO PAGE 16 AND TRY AGAIN

That's right. As a river gets to the end of its journey, it loses the energy to carry mud, silt, and stones. This material, called sediment, is dropped. If it is allowed to build up, sediment can stop the river from being navigable.

Well, you seem to know your stuff, but be careful. The current is strong here and the water level is constantly changing. Do you know why?

WATERWORKS ARE PUMPING IN SEWAGE.
FLIP TO PAGE 28

YOU'RE NEAR THE SEA, SO THE RIVER IS TIDAL.
GO TO PAGE 21

Wrong answer. That might be happening, but it won't affect the currents or water level.

**GO BACK TO PAGE 27
AND THINK AGAIN**

Incorrect.

**GO BACK TO PAGE 15
AND TRY AGAIN**

The Toxic Texter sends back a reply: "Correct. Silt washed downstream by rivers can make rich soils for growing crops. Now paddle downriver to the farm marked F on the map."

Soon you're paddling past fields of cows. Oh no! Someone's dropped an empty plastic barrel in the water. You can't leave trash in the river so you haul it onboard—there's a clue on it!

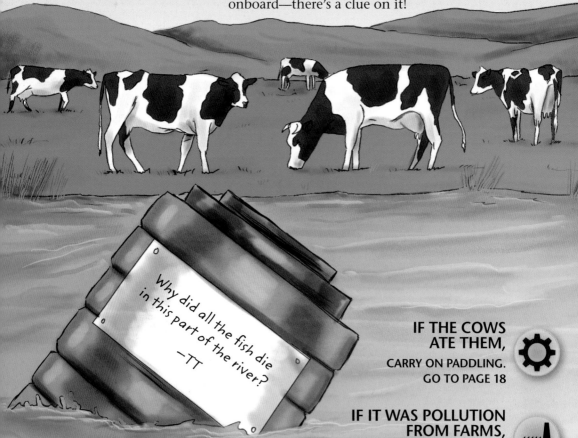

Why did all the fish die in this part of the river?

—TT

**IF THE COWS
ATE THEM,**
CARRY ON PADDLING.
GO TO PAGE 18

**IF IT WAS POLLUTION
FROM FARMS,**
CLIMB ONTO THE RIVERBANK.
TURN TO PAGE 43

That's right. When factories use river water to power or cool machines, dirty water full of chemicals can be pumped back into the river. Serious industrial pollution can kill the animals and plants that live in and beside rivers.

It's getting dark now and you're desperate to get on your way, but the police officer barks:

"Be careful, you fool, get out of the way of that dredger! You know what that is, don't you?"

Think quick! What does a dredger do?

REMOVES MUD AND SAND FROM THE RIVERBED.

HEAD TO PAGE 27

DIGS UP GOLD FROM THE RIVERBED.

GO TO PAGE 36

That's right. An ebb tide means the sea is going out—and your kayak with it. It's too dangerous to plunge into the water after it.

You dash over to the nearby boathouse. The door creaks open. On a table in front of you is a 3D model of the whole river.

A voice booms from a speaker:

Solve this puzzle if you want to save the river. Put the last label in the right place!

Where should you put the "Floodplain" label?

POSITION A.
GO TO PAGE 27 **A**

POSITION B.
TURN TO PAGE 33 **B**

POSITION C.
HEAD TO PAGE 22 **C**

That's right. A new text arrives:

If you want a map to guide you down the river, answer this question: Which is the second longest river in the world?

THE AMAZON RIVER.
GO TO PAGE 32

THE NILE RIVER.
TURN TO PAGE 8

Riversource

A Upstream Tributary

Down-stream

Main river

Meander

C

Wetland

Mouth

B

Floodplain

3 Hooray, you've found the way out! Stalactites are icicle-shaped mineral deposits that hang from the roofs of caves.

You paddle out of the cave and down the river to a reservoir. Suddenly a siren wails. A speedboat surges over and a security guard shouts:

You're under arrest for trespassing! Unless, of course, you're the engineer who's come to examine the dam.

Can you pull this off?
Do you even know what a dam is?

Which is it?

AN ARTIFICIAL LAKE WHERE WATER IS STORED.
TURN TO PAGE 10

A HIGH WALL TO CONTROL THE FLOW OF A RIVER.
GO TO PAGE 15

That's right, the Amazon River in South America comes a close second to the Nile. It's about 4,000 miles long.

Now you've answered the question correctly, the Toxic Texter sends you a map. Your location is shown, and the source of the river is marked with an X.

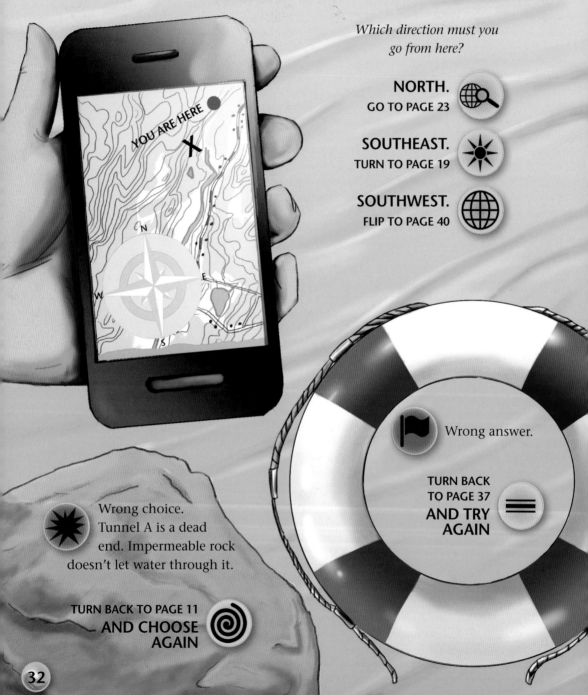

Which direction must you go from here?

NORTH.
GO TO PAGE 23

SOUTHEAST.
TURN TO PAGE 19

SOUTHWEST.
FLIP TO PAGE 40

Wrong answer.

TURN BACK TO PAGE 37 **AND TRY AGAIN**

Wrong choice. Tunnel A is a dead end. Impermeable rock doesn't let water through it.

TURN BACK TO PAGE 11 — **AND CHOOSE AGAIN**

YOU ARE HERE

X

B No, that's a delta (where a river splits into channels at its mouth).

GO BACK TO PAGE 30
AND TRY AGAIN

No, a plain is never V-shaped. A plain is a wide area of flat land.

TURN BACK TO PAGE 8
AND TRY AGAIN

Yes, that's right. Many rivers have been altered by humans so boats can use them safely. Apart from having locks, many rivers are deepened, widened, or straightened.

You notice a trunk beside the lock: it has "TT" on it, like the key the guard gave you. You open it with your key. Inside is a map with an X on a town that's just downriver.

The lockkeeper still won't open the lock gate.

"Answer this question or I won't let you through:"

"Why are many towns and cities beside rivers?"

RIVERS PROVIDE FOOD, DRINKS, AND TRANSPORT.
TURN TO PAGE 42

WHEN RIVERS FREEZE THEY PROVIDE ICE.
FLIP TO PAGE 39

RIVERS ARE GOOD FOR SWIMMING.
GO TO PAGE 19

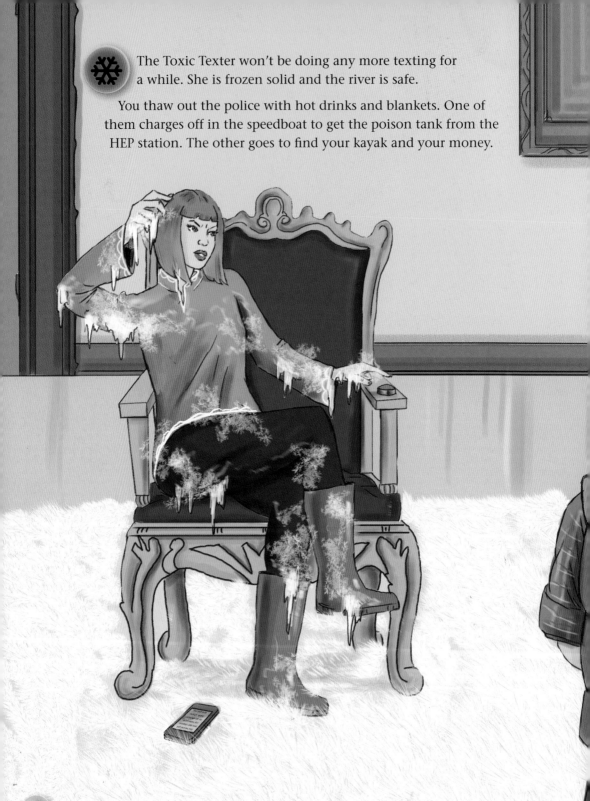

The Toxic Texter won't be doing any more texting for a while. She is frozen solid and the river is safe.

You thaw out the police with hot drinks and blankets. One of them charges off in the speedboat to get the poison tank from the HEP station. The other goes to find your kayak and your money.

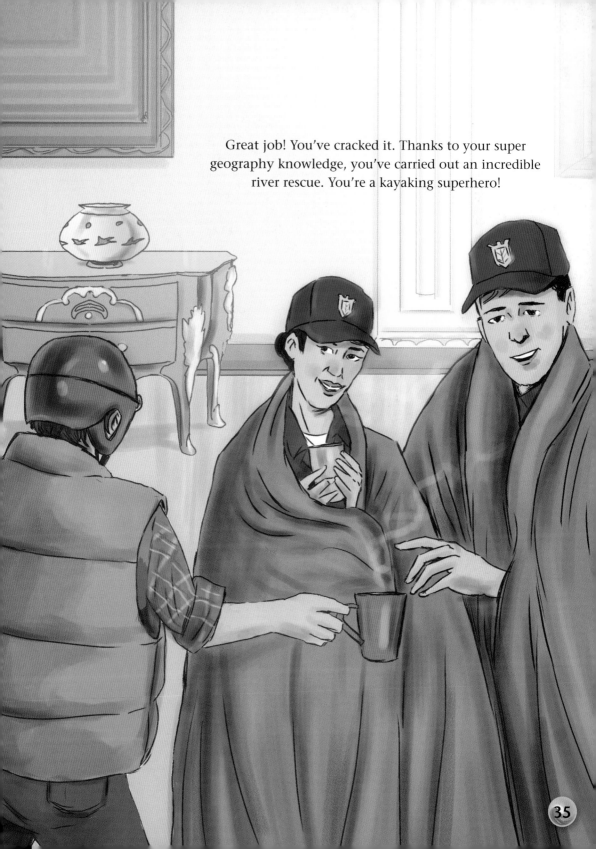

Great job! You've cracked it. Thanks to your super geography knowledge, you've carried out an incredible river rescue. You're a kayaking superhero!

No, a basin is the whole area drained by a river.

TURN BACK TO PAGE 10 AND TRY AGAIN

C Wrong rope.

TURN BACK TO PAGE 5 AND TRY AGAIN

Correct. In this hydroelectric power station, the river is held behind the dam in a reservoir. Water is released through the dam at great force, spinning blades on a turbine. This energy makes electricity.

"The dam looks great," you stutter. *"I think I'll be off now."*

That's not what dredgers do!

TURN BACK TO PAGE 29 AND HAVE ANOTHER TRY

That was quick. I'm not sure about you. Answer this question correctly or I'll call the police.

What do we call hydroelectric power?

GREEN ENERGY.
FLIP TO PAGE 38

POLLUTING ENERGY.
GO TO PAGE 23

Incorrect. Weathering is the breaking down of rocks by rain, wind, and freezing—not by rivers.

GO BACK TO PAGE 13 FOR ANOTHER TRY

Wrong choice. The Niagara Falls (on the border between Canada and the United States) are actually three waterfalls, but they are only 167 feet high.

TURN TO PAGE 17 AND TRY AGAIN

That's right. Locks are like miniature dams with gates. A series of locks can form a "staircase" where the river flows downhill. When the lock gates close, the water level inside is raised or lowered.

You paddle downstream until you see a lock.
"*You have to pay to come through here,*"
yells the lockkeeper.

You explain you don't have any money.

You can pay me with the correct answer to this question. Locks make rivers navigable, but what does navigable mean?

USED BY THE NAVY.
GO TO PAGE 32

EASY FOR BOATS TO SAIL ALONG.
GO TO PAGE 33

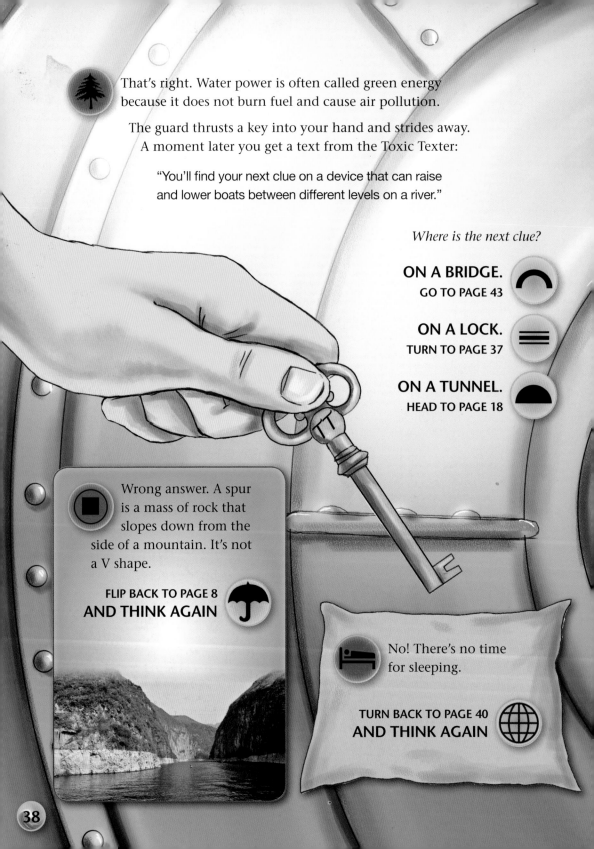

That's right. Water power is often called green energy because it does not burn fuel and cause air pollution.

The guard thrusts a key into your hand and strides away. A moment later you get a text from the Toxic Texter:

"You'll find your next clue on a device that can raise and lower boats between different levels on a river."

Where is the next clue?

ON A BRIDGE.
GO TO PAGE 43

ON A LOCK.
TURN TO PAGE 37

ON A TUNNEL.
HEAD TO PAGE 18

Wrong answer. A spur is a mass of rock that slopes down from the side of a mountain. It's not a V shape.

FLIP BACK TO PAGE 8
AND THINK AGAIN

No! There's no time for sleeping.

TURN BACK TO PAGE 40
AND THINK AGAIN

That's not
the reason.

**GO BACK
TO PAGE 33
AND THINK
AGAIN**

 Nope. Although storms, floods,
and strong winds have worn away
some of the Grand Canyon, they
weren't the main force that carved
the feature.

**GO BACK TO PAGE 41
FOR ANOTHER TRY**

A That's the right answer. A
watershed is an area of higher
ground that divides river
basins (the areas that drain water
into a river).

When you haul on rope A,
there is a message attached:

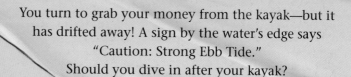

Come to the old
boathouse.

You turn to grab your money from the kayak—but it
has drifted away! A sign by the water's edge says
"Caution: Strong Ebb Tide."
Should you dive in after your kayak?

What does "ebb tide" mean?

**YOUR KAYAK WILL
DRIFT OUT TO SEA.**
GO TO PAGE 30

**YOUR KAYAK WILL
COME IN WITH THE TIDE.**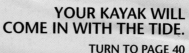
TURN TO PAGE 40

**CAUTION:
STRONG
EBB TIDE**

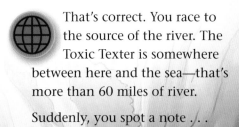 That's correct. You race to the source of the river. The Toxic Texter is somewhere between here and the sea—that's more than 60 miles of river.

Suddenly, you spot a note . . .

 Unfortunately not!

TURN BACK TO PAGE 39 AND TRY AGAIN A

You've made it to the start of the Treasure Hunt —or should I say Poison Hunt? Now go to bed!

—TT

It's a riddle, but what does it mean?

LIE DOWN ON THE BANK FOR A NAP.
TURN TO PAGE 38

GO AND EXAMINE THE SPRING.
HEAD TO PAGE 21

WADE INTO THE STREAM.
GO TO PAGE 16

Smoke *is* air pollution, but that's not what the officer meant.

GO BACK TO PAGE 20 AND THINK AGAIN

Correct choice.

You paddle downstream in the kayak. After a few miles, you flop onto the riverbank for a rest. *"What are you doing?"* a woman shouts. *"This river flows through my land!"* She grabs your kayak.

You explain you're an explorer on a mission, but she doesn't believe you.

Wrong answer!

TURN BACK TO PAGE 42 AND TRY AGAIN

Prove you're an explorer or I won't let you get back in your kayak. I grew up in the United States, near the Grand Canyon. What carved out the Grand Canyon?

AN EARTHQUAKE.
TURN TO PAGE 5

THE COLORADO RIVER.
GO TO PAGE 13

STORMS AND TORNADOES.
FLIP TO PAGE 39

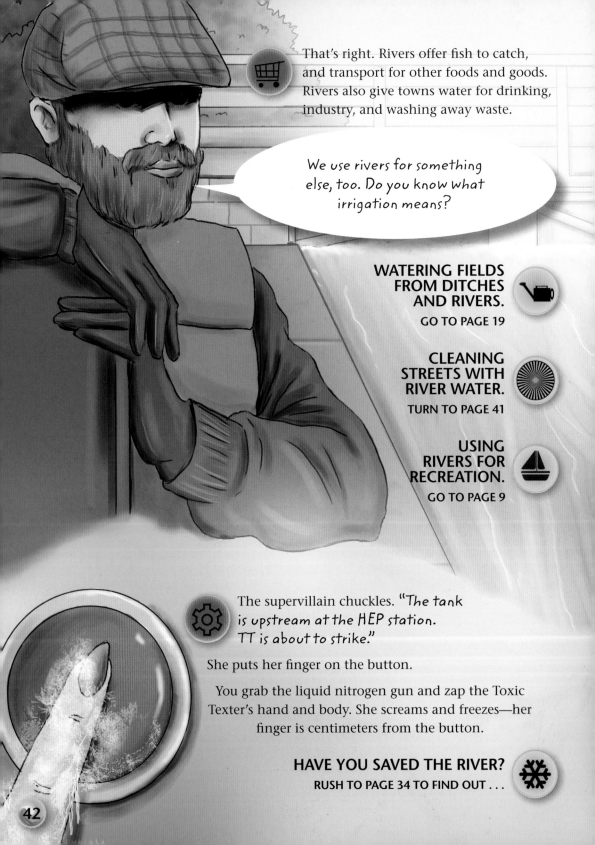

That's right. Rivers offer fish to catch, and transport for other foods and goods. Rivers also give towns water for drinking, industry, and washing away waste.

We use rivers for something else, too. Do you know what irrigation means?

WATERING FIELDS FROM DITCHES AND RIVERS.
GO TO PAGE 19

CLEANING STREETS WITH RIVER WATER.
TURN TO PAGE 41

USING RIVERS FOR RECREATION.
GO TO PAGE 9

The supervillain chuckles. "The tank is upstream at the HEP station. TT is about to strike."

She puts her finger on the button.

You grab the liquid nitrogen gun and zap the Toxic Texter's hand and body. She screams and freezes—her finger is centimeters from the button.

HAVE YOU SAVED THE RIVER?
RUSH TO PAGE 34 TO FIND OUT . . .

That's right. Chemicals used in farming, such as fertilizers and pesticides, can wash into rivers and pollute them, killing plants and animals.

You climb onto the riverbank. Yikes, there's a huge bull! You're about to leap back into the kayak, when you see a label around its neck. You quickly read the note . . .

Paddle past the tributary.

—TT

Wrong choice. For once, the Toxic Texter wasn't tricking you.

TURN BACK TO PAGE 12 AND TRY AGAIN

No, that's not right. Bridges are built so people and goods can get across rivers.

TURN BACK TO PAGE 38 AND TRY AGAIN

What's a tributary?

POLLUTION FROM TOILETS AND FACTORIES.

HEAD TO PAGE 26

WHERE A RIVER MEETS THE SEA.

GO TO PAGE 5

A RIVER THAT FLOWS INTO ANOTHER RIVER.

FLIP TO PAGE 20

GLOSSARY

Alluvium

Material made of silt, sand, clay, and gravel, which is deposited by rivers.

Buoy

An anchored object that floats on water to mark a channel or warn of danger.

Canyon

A deep, narrow valley with steep sides, often with water flowing through it.

Condense

To turn a gas into a liquid (condensation). When water vapor in the air gets cold, it changes back into liquid that falls as rain.

Current

The flow of water along a river, which is affected by the steepness of the slope, the shape of the channel, and the amount of water flowing through it. Near the sea, the current in rivers can reverse when the tide changes.

Deposition

The leaving behind of material. When a river loses energy, it will drop or deposit some of the material it is carrying. This often happens when a river enters an area of shallow water or when the volume of water decreases, as may happen after a flood. Deposition happens mostly toward the end of a river's journey, at the river mouth.

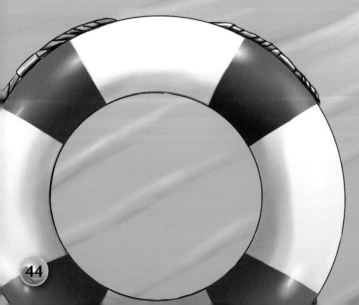

Erosion

The wearing away of rock and soil, as often happens along a riverbed and banks. Erosion also breaks down the rock particles being carried downstream by a river.

Estuary

The tidal mouth of a river, with flat stretches of mud exposed at low tide.

Evaporate

To turn from a liquid into a gas. When the sun heats up water in rivers, lakes, or the ocean, some of it turns into vapor or steam, which rises into the air as invisible gas.

Floodplain

The wide, flat floor of a river valley. It is covered by layers of sediments (alluvium) deposited by the river after flooding.

Gorge

A steep-sided, narrow, rocky valley.

Kayak

A canoe of a type first used by Inuit people. It is made of a light frame with a watertight covering that has a small opening in the top to sit in.

Liquid nitrogen

Nitrogen becomes a liquid at -346°F. It looks like water but is so cold, it immediately freezes skin on contact.

Meander

A bend or loop in a river. The water on the outside of the bend cuts into the bank, eroding it and making a river cliff. At the same time, the slower-moving water on the inside of the bend deposits material.

Oxbow lake

A horseshoe-shaped lake left behind where a river once flowed in a meander.

Permeable

Allowing fluids and gases to pass through. Rocks through which water can pass are described as permeable. Cracks or pores in the rock allow liquids or gases to pass through them. The opposite of permeable is impermeable.

Plunge pool

A deep pool below a waterfall.

Pollution

The spoiling or contamination of the environment (such as the air, water, or soil).

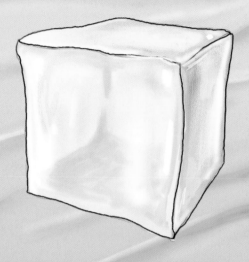

Rapids

A fast-flowing, shallow stretch of "white water" where a river flows over hard rock.

Reservoir

A lake where water is collected and stored as a water supply.

Stalactite

A pointed column hanging down from the roof of a cave, formed over hundreds of years by dripping water. Minerals in the water are left behind as it drops slowly from the roof.

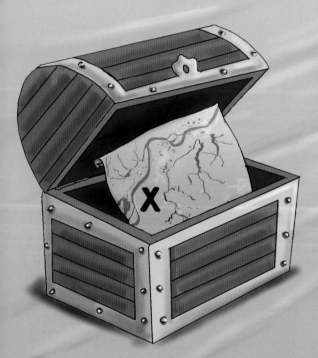

Stalagmite

A pointed column growing up from the floor of a cave, formed by water containing minerals that drops from a stalactite over hundreds of years.

Swallow hole

A hole in the ground linked to an underground passage (especially in limestone), formed by erosion and the collapse of a cavern roof.

Tidal

Where the flow and depth of a river is affected by seawater as the tide rises or falls.

Turbine

An engine with a central driving shaft that has a series of blades spun around by the pressure of water, steam, or air.

Water vapor

Water when it is in the atmosphere as a gas, as in clouds.

Whirlpool

Where water swirls rapidly in a circle. Floating objects are pulled into a hollow in the center of the circle.

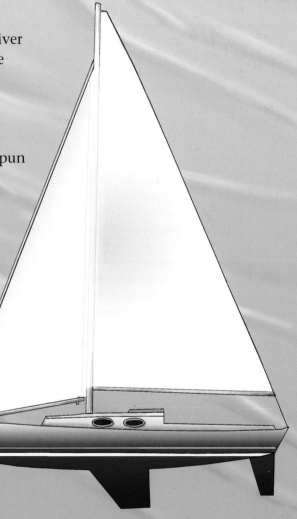

Taking it further

The Geography Quest books are designed to inspire children to develop and apply their geographical knowledge through compelling adventure stories. For each story, children must solve a series of problems and challenges on their way to completing an exciting quest.

The books do not follow a page-by-page order. The reader jumps forward and backward through the book according to the answers given to the problems. If his or her answers are correct, the reader progresses to the next part of the story; incorrect answers are fully explained before the reader is directed back to attempt the problem once again.

Additional help may be found in the glossary at the back of the book.

To support the development of your child's geographical knowledge, you can:

⛵ Read the book with your child.

⛵ Continue reading with your child until he or she is using the book confidently, following the "Go to" instructions to the next puzzle or explanation.

⛵ Encourage your child to read on alone. Prompt your child to tell you how the story is developing, and what problems they have solved.

⛵ Point out the differences and similarities between landscapes and conditions in different parts of the world. Talk about how weather and rivers (drainage) have a major impact on human activities.

⛵ Discuss what it would be like to kayak from the source of a river all the way to its mouth. What would be the dangers, as well as the changes, in the river along its journey?

⛵ Take advantage of the many sources of geographical and meteorological information, such as libraries, museums and documentaries. The Internet is another valuable resource, and there is plenty of material aimed at children. Be careful only to visit websites endorsed by respected educational authorities, such as museums and universities.

⛵ Remember, we learn most when we're enjoying ourselves, so make geography fun!